Great Works

Instructional Guides for Literature

The Outsiders

A guide for the novel by S.E. Hinton
Great Works Author: Wendy Conklin

SHELL EDUCATION

Publishing Credits

Robin Erickson, *Production Director*; Lee Aucoin, *Creative Director*; Timothy J. Bradley, *Illustration Manager*; Emily R. Smith, M.A.Ed., *Editorial Director*; Jill K. Mulhall, M.Ed., *Editor*; Amber Goff, *Editorial Assistant*; Don Tran, *Production Supervisor*; Corinne Burton, M.A.Ed., *Publisher*

Image Credits

Sunset Boulevard/Corbis (cover)

Standards

© 2007 Teachers of English to Speakers of Other Languages, Inc. (TESOL)
© 2007 Board of Regents of the University of Wisconsin System. World-Class Instructional Design and Assessment (WIDA)
© Copyright 2010 National Governors Association Center for Best Practices and Council of Chief State School Officers. All rights reserved

---

Shell Education

5301 Oceanus Drive
Huntington Beach, CA 92649-1030
http://www.shelleducation.com
ISBN 978-1-4258-8995-1
© 2014 Shell Educational Publishing, Inc.

Table of Contents

How to Use This Literature Guide

Today's standards demand rigor and relevance in the reading of complex texts. The units in this series guide teachers in a rich and deep exploration of worthwhile works of literature for classroom study. The most rigorous instruction can also be interesting and engaging!

Many current strategies for effective literacy instruction have been incorporated into these instructional guides for literature. Throughout the units, text-dependent questions are used to determine comprehension of the book as well as student interpretation of the vocabulary words. The books chosen for the series are complex exemplars of carefully crafted works of literature. Close reading is used throughout the units to guide students toward revisiting the text and using textual evidence to respond to prompts orally and in writing. Students must analyze the story elements in multiple assignments for each section of the book. All of these strategies work together to rigorously guide students through their study of literature.

The next few pages will make clear how to use this guide for a purposeful and meaningful literature study. Each section of this guide is set up in the same way to make it easier for you to implement the instruction in your classroom.

Theme Thoughts

The great works of literature used throughout this series have important themes that have been relevant to people for many years. Many of the themes will be discussed during the various sections of this instructional guide. However, it would also benefit students to have independent time to think about the key themes of the novel.

Before students begin reading, have them complete *Pre-Reading Theme Thoughts* (page 13). This graphic organizer will allow students to think about the themes outside the context of the story. They'll have the opportunity to evaluate statements based on important themes and defend their opinions. Be sure to have students keep their papers for comparison to the *Post-Reading Theme Thoughts* (page 64). This graphic organizer is similar to the pre-reading activity. However, this time, students will be answering the questions from the point of view of one of the characters of the novel. They have to think about how the character would feel about each statement and defend their thoughts. To conclude the activity, have students compare what they thought about the themes before they read the novel to what the characters discovered during the story.

How to Use This Literature Guide (cont.)

Vocabulary

Each teacher overview page has definitions and sentences about how key vocabulary words are used in the section. These words should be introduced and discussed with students. There are two student vocabulary activity pages in each section. On the first page, students are asked to define the ten words chosen by the author of this unit. On the second page in most sections, each student will select at least eight words that he or she finds interesting or difficult. For each section, choose one of these pages for your students to complete. With either assignment, you may want to have students get into pairs to discuss the meanings of the words. Allow students to use reference guides to define the words. Monitor students to make sure the definitions they have found are accurate and relate to how the words are used in the text.

On some of the vocabulary student pages, students are asked to answer text-related questions about the vocabulary words. The following question stems will help you create your own vocabulary questions if you'd like to extend the discussion.

- How does this word describe _____'s character?
- In what ways does this word relate to the problem in this story?
- How does this word help you understand the setting?
- In what ways is this word related to the story's solution?
- Describe how this word supports the novel's theme of . . . .
- What visual images does this word bring to your mind?
- For what reasons might the author have chosen to use this particular word?

At times, more work with the words will help students understand their meanings. The following quick vocabulary activities are a good way to further study the words.

- Have students practice their vocabulary and writing skills by creating sentences and/or paragraphs in which multiple vocabulary words are used correctly and with evidence of understanding.
- Students can play vocabulary concentration. Students make a set of cards with the words and a separate set of cards with the definitions. Then, students lay the cards out on the table and play concentration. The goal of the game is to match vocabulary words with their definitions.
- Students can create word journal entries about the words. Students choose words they think are important and then describe why they think each word is important within the novel.

How to Use This Literature Guide (cont.)

Analyzing the Literature

After students have read each section, hold small-group or whole-class discussions. Questions are written at two levels of complexity to allow you to decide which questions best meet the needs of your students. The Level 1 questions are typically less abstract than the Level 2 questions. Level 1 is indicated by a square, while Level 2 is indicated by a triangle.

These questions focus on the various story elements, such as character, setting, and plot. Student pages are provided if you want to assign these questions for individual student work before your group discussion. Be sure to add further questions as your students discuss what they've read. For each question, a few key points are provided for your reference as you discuss the novel with students.

Reader Response

In today's classrooms, there are often great readers who are below average writers. So much time and energy is spent in classrooms getting students to read on grade level, that little time is left to focus on writing skills. To help teachers include more writing in their daily literacy instruction, each section of this guide has a literature-based reader response prompt. Each of the three genres of writing is used in the reader responses within this guide: narrative, informative/explanatory, and argument. Students have a choice between two prompts for each reader response. One response requires students to make connections between the reading and their own lives. The other prompt requires students to determine text-to-text connections or connections within the text.

Close Reading the Literature

Within each section, students are asked to closely reread a short section of text. Since some versions of the novels have different page numbers, the selections are described by chapter and location, along with quotations to guide the readers. After each close reading, there are text-dependent questions to be answered by students.

Encourage students to read each question one at a time and then go back to the text and discover the answer. Work with students to ensure that they use the text to determine their answers rather than making unsupported inferences. Once students have answered the questions, discuss what they discovered. Suggested answers are provided in the answer key.

How to Use This Literature Guide (cont.)

Close Reading the Literature (cont.)

The generic, open-ended stems below can be used to write your own text-dependent questions if you would like to give students more practice.

- Give evidence from the text to support . . . .
- Justify your thinking using text evidence about . . . .
- Find evidence to support your conclusions about . . . .
- What text evidence helps the reader understand . . . ?
- Use the book to tell why _____ happens.
- Based on events in the story, ...
- Use text evidence to describe why . . . .

Making Connections

The activities in this section help students make cross-curricular connections to writing, mathematics, science, social studies, or the fine arts. Each of these types of activities requires higher-order thinking skills from students.

Creating with the Story Elements

It is important to spend time discussing the common story elements in literature. Understanding the characters, setting, and plot can increase students' comprehension and appreciation of the story. If teachers discuss these elements daily, students will more likely internalize the concepts and look for the elements in their independent reading. Another important reason for focusing on the story elements is that students will be better writers if they think about how the stories they read are constructed.

Students are given three options for working with the story elements. They are asked to create something related to the characters, setting, or plot of the novel. Students are given a choice on this activity so that they can decide to complete the activity that most appeals to them. Different multiple intelligences are used so that the activities are diverse and interesting to all students.

How to Use This Literature Guide (cont.)

Culminating Activity

This open-ended, cross-curricular activity requires higher-order thinking and allows for a creative product. Students will enjoy getting the chance to share what they have discovered through reading the novel. Be sure to allow them enough time to complete the activity at school or home.

Comprehension Assessment

The questions in this section are modeled after current standardized tests to help students analyze what they've read and prepare for tests they may see in their classrooms. The questions are dependent on the text and require critical-thinking skills to answer.

Response to Literature

The final post-reading activity is an essay based on the text that also requires further research by students. This is a great way to extend this book into other curricular areas. A suggested rubric is provided for teacher reference.

Correlation to the Standards

Shell Education is committed to producing educational materials that are research and standards based. As part of this effort, we have correlated all of our products to the academic standards of all 50 states, the District of Columbia, the Department of Defense Dependents Schools, and all Canadian provinces.

Purpose and Intent of Standards

Standards are designed to focus instruction and guide adoption of curricula. Standards are statements that describe the criteria necessary for students to meet specific academic goals. They define the knowledge, skills, and content students should acquire at each level. Standards are also used to develop standardized tests to evaluate students' academic progress. Teachers are required to demonstrate how their lessons meet standards. Standards are used in the development of all of our products, so educators can be assured they meet high academic standards.

How to Find Standards Correlations

To print a customized correlation report of this product for your state, visit our website at http://www.shelleducation.com and follow the online directions. If you require assistance in printing correlation reports, please contact our Customer Service Department at 1-877-777-3450.

Correlation to the Standards (cont.)

Standards Correlation Chart

The lessons in this guide were written to support the Common Core College and Career Readiness Anchor Standards. This chart indicates which sections of this guide address the anchor standards.

Common Core College and Career Readiness Anchor Standard	Section
CCSS.ELA-Literacy.CCRA.R.1—Read closely to determine what the text says explicitly and to make logical inferences from it; cite specific textual evidence when writing or speaking to support conclusions drawn from the text.	Analyzing the Literature Sections 1–5; Close Reading the Literature Sections 1–5; Making Connections Sections 4–5; Creating with the Story Elements Sections 1–5; Culminating Activity
CCSS.ELA-Literacy.CCRA.R.2—Determine central ideas or themes of a text and analyze their development; summarize the key supporting details and ideas.	Analyzing the Literature Sections 1–5; Making Connections Sections 1, 3–5; Creating with the Story Elements Sections 1, 4–5; Post-Reading Theme Thoughts; Culminating Activity; Post-Reading Response to Literature
CCSS.ELA-Literacy.CCRA.R.3—Analyze how and why individuals, events, or ideas develop and interact over the course of a text.	Analyzing the Literature Sections 1–5; Close Reading the Literature Sections 1–5; Post-Reading Theme Thoughts
CCSS.ELA-Literacy.CCRA.R.4—Interpret words and phrases as they are used in a text, including determining technical, connotative, and figurative meanings, and analyze how specific word choices shape meaning or tone.	Vocabulary Sections 1–5; Creating with the Story Elements Section 2
CCSS.ELA-Literacy.CCRA.R.5—Analyze the structure of texts, including how specific sentences, paragraphs, and larger portions of the text (e.g., a section, chapter, scene, or stanza) relate to each other and the whole.	Post-Reading Response to Literature
CCSS.ELA-Literacy.CCRA.R.6—Assess how point of view or purpose shapes the content and style of a text.	Creating with the Story Elements Sections 1, 3–4; Making Connections Section 2; Culminating Activity; Post-Reading Theme Thoughts
CCSS.ELA-Literacy.CCRA.W.1—Write arguments to support claims in an analysis of substantive topics or texts using valid reasoning and relevant and sufficient evidence.	Reader Response Sections 1–2, 5; Creating with the Story Elements Section 5; Making Connections Section 5; Post-Reading Response to Literature
CCSS.ELA-Literacy.CCRA.W.2—Write informative/explanatory texts to examine and convey complex ideas and information clearly and accurately through the effective selection, organization, and analysis of content.	Reader Response Sections 1, 3–5; Making Connections Sections 1, 3; Post-Reading Response to Literature
CCSS.ELA-Literacy.CCRA.W.3—Write narratives to develop real or imagined experiences or events using effective technique, well-chosen details and well-structured event sequences.	Reader Response Sections 2–4; Creating with the Story Elements Sections 1, 3–4

Correlation to the Standards (cont.)

Standards Correlation Chart (cont.)

Common Core College and Career Readiness Anchor Standard	Section
CCSS.ELA-Literacy.CCRA.W.4—Produce clear and coherent writing in which the development, organization, and style are appropriate to task, purpose, and audience.	Reader Response Sections 2–4; Making Connections Sections 1, 3; Creating with the Story Elements Sections 1, 3–4; Post-Reading Response to Literature
CCSS.ELA-Literacy.CCRA.W.6—Use technology, including the Internet, to produce and publish writing and to interact and collaborate with others.	Creating with the Story Elements Sections 1–2, 5; Culminating Activity
CCSS.ELA-Literacy.CCRA.W.9—Draw evidence from literary or informational texts to support analysis, reflection, and research.	Close Reading the Literature Sections 1–5; Making Connections Sections 1, 3–5
CCSS.ELA-Literacy.CCRA.L.1—Demonstrate command of the conventions of standard English grammar and usage when writing or speaking.	Making Connections Sections 1, 3; Culminating Activity; Post-Reading Response to Literature
CCSS.ELA-Literacy.CCRA.L.4—Determine or clarify the meaning of unknown and multiple-meaning words and phrases by using context clues, analyzing meaningful word parts, and consulting general and specialized reference materials, as appropriate.	Vocabulary Sections 1–5
CCSS.ELA-Literacy.CCRA.L.6—Acquire and use accurately a range of general academic and domain-specific words and phrases sufficient for reading, writing, speaking, and listening at the college and career readiness level; demonstrate independence in gathering vocabulary knowledge when encountering an unknown term important to comprehension or expression.	Vocabulary Sections 1–5

TESOL and WIDA Standards

The lessons in this book promote English language development for English language learners. The following TESOL and WIDA English Language Development Standards are addressed through the activities in this book:

- **Standard 1:** English language learners communicate for social and instructional purposes within the school setting.

- **Standard 2:** English language learners communicate information, ideas and concepts necessary for academic success in the content area of language arts.

About the Author—S.E. Hinton

From a really young age, Susan Eloise Hinton (S.E. Hinton) knew she wanted to be a writer. She spent many years practicing her skills and reading voraciously. After one of her friends was badly beaten by a group of wealthier teenagers, she began writing *The Outsiders*—mainly to blow off steam about the incident. She was only fifteen years old at the time and never intended for that piece of writing to become a book, but she continued writing and finished the story the following year.

Part of her drive to finish the book was a desire to convey what life was like from a unique perspective. At the time all the books on the shelves for young adults were unrealistic, in her mind. They didn't tell the real story of what was going on with teenagers. Even though she never believed it would be published, she had to get her story on paper. Writing was her therapy and helped her deal with the complications of teenage life.

While at school one day, Hinton told a friend that she had written this story. The friend's mother was a writer of children's books, and she passed the book along to someone who had an agent in New York. As luck would have it, Hinton was offered a publishing contract on the day she graduated from high school.

Because her publisher feared what others might think about a girl writing a book like *The Outsiders*, Hinton used her initials when she published the book, instead of her full name. Hinton grew to like the fact that she had a pen name. This pen name enabled her to live a private life in Tulsa, Oklahoma, the actual, unstated setting of *The Outsiders*.

In 1983, Francis Ford Coppola directed the movie version of *The Outsiders*. He consulted Hinton every step of the way to make sure that the visual representation of this story met her standards and vision as the author. The movie starred many young, up-and-coming actors and helped to bring new popularity to the novel.

After writing *The Outsiders*, Hinton published several other young adult novels, including *That Was Then, This Is Now* and *Rumble Fish* as well as a few stories for young children, including *The Puppy Sister*. Even though it has been decades since Hinton wrote *The Outsiders*, she still receives letters from fans telling her how her story has touched their lives. For her personally, writing the story was just a way to cope with a very difficult time in her life. But she is grateful that it has helped so many others and continues to affect young people today.

Possible Texts for Text Comparisons

The author makes comparisons in the story using scenes from *Gone with the Wind* by Margaret Mitchell and Jack London's wolf books (such as *White Fang* and *The Call of the Wild*). Selections from both of these texts can be used to discuss themes of survival or compare how the gangs fight one another.

Book Summary of *The Outsiders*

Set in Tulsa, Oklahoma, *The Outsiders* tells a story about the divisions of social class amongst high school students in the 1960s. The story is narrated by sensitive 14-year-old Ponyboy, an orphan who is being raised by his two older brothers. Ponyboy's gang is made up of tough kids called greasers, after the oil they wear in their hair. They rival the Socs, pronounced SOSH-ehs (short for Socials), who are the rich kids across town. Both of these groups attend the same high school, but they have very different lives.

The story begins with Ponyboy getting "jumped" by a group of Socs while he is walking home alone from the movies. His gang shows up and saves him, but Ponyboy is shaken by the experience. He struggles to understand why this happens and why there has to be such a division between the social classes. Later, Ponyboy meets a Soc girl name of them form a connection. She begins to change his preconceived judgment that all Socs have it made because they have money, good clothes, and nice cars.

Through a series of terrible events, Ponyboy and his good friend Johnny find themselves on the run and hiding from the law in an old church. A fellow greaser helps them, and just when Ponyboy and Johnny decide to turn themselves in, a fire in the church changes the sequence of events. The boys work to save young children caught in the fire, but they are hurt in the process.

Ponyboy returns home, where social tensions run high, and has a further encounter with a Soc who opens up and shares his perspectives with Ponyboy. Ponyboy internalizes these encounters and tries to make sense of how society functions while also working to cope with his own home life and his two older brothers.

The story concludes with Ponyboy coming to the understanding that things are "rough all over" and deciding to tell his story in the hope it will give others a new perspective on society's outsiders.

Cross-Curricular Connection

This story can be used to make connections in history concerning the social classes and divisions in most societies over the course of time. The book is also good for discussions about preconceived judgments and biases in a philosophy course.

Possible Texts for Text Sets

- Austen, Jane. *Sense and Sensibility*. HarperCollins Publishers, 2013.
- Hosseini, Khaled. *The Kite Runner*. Riverhead, 2004.
- Roth, Veronica. *Divergent*. Katherine Tegen Books, 2011.

Name _____

Date _____

Pre-Reading Theme Thoughts

Directions: Read each of the statements in the first column. Decide if you agree or disagree with the statements. Record your opinion by marking an X in Agree or Disagree for each statement. Explain your choices in the fourth column. There are no right or wrong answers.

Statement	Agree	Disagree	Explain Your Answer
Rich people have just as many worries as poor people.			
It is better to grow up too fast than to be treated like a child.			
People judge others by their appearances.			
Sometimes, life isn't fair.			

Vocabulary Overview

Ten key words from this section are provided below with definitions and sentences about how the words are used in the book. Choose one of the vocabulary activity sheets (pages 15 or 16) for students to complete as they read this section. Monitor students as they work to ensure the definitions they have found are accurate and relate to the text. Finally, discuss these important vocabulary words with students. If you think these words or other words in the section warrant more time devoted to them, there are suggestions in the introduction for other vocabulary activities (page 5).

Word or Phrase	Definition	Sentence about Text
madras (ch. 1)	a light cotton fabric, usually with a colorful pattern	The Soc that threatens to cut off Ponyboy's hair wears a blue **madras** shirt.
bleedin' like a stuck pig (ch. 1)	bleeding profusely	After the Soc cuts him, Ponyboy **bleeds like a stuck pig**.
hence (ch. 1)	for this reason	Two-Bit always has to get his two-bits in. **Hence** his self-explanatory nickname.
out of the cooler (ch. 1)	out of jail	Dally got **out of the cooler** early because of good behavior.
rolled (ch. 1)	robbed	Dally **rolled** a drunk senior to get the ring that he wears.
savvy (ch. 1)	understand	Even though you think Darry is too hard on you, he only acts that way because he loves you a lot. **Savvy**?
fuzz (ch. 2)	a slang term for the police	The **fuzz** always shows up when the switchblades come out.
coolly (ch. 2)	calmly and under control	Dally eyes the Soc girls **coolly** before taking the seat right behind them.
roguishly (ch. 2)	mischievously	Dally, known for playing jokes, smiles **roguishly**.
incredulous (ch. 2)	disbelieving; skeptical	Cherry gives Dally an **incredulous** look and throws a soda in his face.

Name _____

Date _____

Understanding Vocabulary Words

Directions: The following words appear in this section of the book. Use context clues and reference materials to determine an accurate definition for each word.

Word or Phrase	Definition
madras (ch. 1)	
bleedin' like a stuck pig (ch. 1)	
hence (ch. 1)	
out of the cooler (ch. 1)	
rolled (ch. 1)	
savvy (ch. 1)	
fuzz (ch. 2)	
coolly (ch. 2)	
roguishly (ch. 2)	
incredulous (ch. 2)	

Name _____

Date _____

During-Reading Vocabulary Activity

Directions: As you read these chapters, record at least eight important words on the lines below. Try to find interesting, difficult, intriguing, special, or funny words. Your words can be long or short. They can be hard or easy to spell. After each word, use context clues in the text and reference materials to define the word.

- _____
- _____
- _____
- _____
- _____
- _____
- _____
- _____
- _____
- _____

Directions: Respond to the following questions about the words in this section.

1. Why is it fitting that, out of all the greasers, Dally is the one who is described as smiling **roguishly**?

   _____

   _____

2. Why do you think the greasers use the word **heater** as slang for a handgun?

   _____

   _____

Analyzing the Literature

Provided below are discussion questions you can use in small groups, with the whole class, or for written assignments. Each question is given at two levels so you can choose the right question for each group of students. Activity sheets with these questions are provided (pages 18–19) if you want students to write their responses. For each question, a few key discussion points are provided for your reference.

Story Element	■ Level 1	▲ Level 2	Key Discussion Points
Character	Why do Darry and Ponyboy have trouble getting along? Find clues in the text to support your thinking.	Why is the relationship between Darry and Ponyboy a complicated one? Does it have to be that way? Support your answers with references to the text.	Discuss the tremendous weight Darry must feel as the oldest brother, having had to take on more responsibility with the death of their parents. Talk about Ponyboy's immaturity at his age. Be sure to discuss the end of chapter 1 where Ponyboy lies to himself about how he feels about Darry.
Setting	What specific words, phrases, and scenes in the text tell you that this novel was written long ago?	This novel was written several decades ago. What clues indicate that it is not set in the present day?	Have students point to various phrases in the text like "just didn't dig each other" and "Get lost, hood!" There are also outmoded settings like the drive-in movie theater and the DX station.
Plot	Ponyboy is hurt by the Socs in chapter 1. Why does the author have this happen so early in the book?	The Socs beat up Ponyboy at the very beginning of the novel. Why does the author choose to open the novel with this incident?	Talk about how the author wants the readers to "experience" this violence early on, instead of just reading about when Johnny was jumped. The author is setting the stage for the upcoming clash between the Socs and the greasers.
Character	In what ways are Cherry and Marcia different from each other?	Marcia does not see any reason to throw away a perfectly good, free soda while Cherry throws hers away based on "the principle of the matter." What do these actions tell us about these two characters?	Clues show that Cherry is sensitive to others' feelings. She stops Marcia from saying Johnny and Ponyboy look 14. She notices that Johnny must have been hurt at some time in his past. Marcia is content to have fun with Two-Bit during the movie. She appears to be practical because she doesn't want to waste a soda, while Cherry has principles that matter to her.

Name _____

Date _____

■ Analyzing the Literature

Directions: Think about the section you just read. Read each question and provide a response that includes textual evidence.

1. Why do Darry and Ponyboy have trouble getting along? Find clues in the text to support your thinking.

   _____

   _____

   _____

   _____

2. What specific words, phrases, and scenes in the text tell you that this novel was written long ago?

   _____

   _____

   _____

   _____

3. Ponyboy is hurt by the Socs in chapter 1. Why does the author have this happen so early in the book?

   _____

   _____

   _____

   _____

4. In what ways are Cherry and Marcia different from each other?

   _____

   _____

   _____

Name _____

Date _____

▲ Analyzing the Literature

Directions: Think about the section you just read. Read each question and provide a response that includes textual evidence.

1. Why is the relationship between Darry and Ponyboy a complicated one? Does it have to be that way? Support your answers with references to the text.

   _____

   _____

   _____

2. This novel was written several decades ago. What clues indicate that it is not set in the present day?

   _____

   _____

   _____

3. The Socs beat up Ponyboy at the very beginning of the novel. Why does the author choose to open the novel with this incident?

   _____

   _____

   _____

   _____

4. Marcia does not see any reason to throw away a perfectly good, free soda while Cherry throws hers away based on "the principle of the matter." What do these actions tell us about these two characters?

   _____

   _____

   _____

Name _____

Date _____

Reader Response

Directions: Choose one of the following prompts about this section to answer. Be sure you include a topic sentence in your response, use textual evidence to support your opinion, and provide a strong conclusion that summarizes your opinion.

Writing Prompts

- **Informative/Explanatory Piece**—What similarities and differences does your school or community have with Ponyboy's community?
- **Argument Piece**—In what ways does S.E. Hinton provide information and details that make the story seem realistic to readers?

_____

_____

_____

_____

_____

_____

_____

_____

_____

_____

_____

_____

_____

_____

_____

_____

_____

Name _____

Date _____

Close Reading the Literature

Directions: Closely reread the section at the end of chapter 1 beginning with "Darry didn't deserve to work like an old man . . . ." Continue reading until the end of the chapter. Read each question below and then revisit the text to find evidence that supports your answer.

1. Use clues from the text to describe how Darry's life could have been different if his parents had not died in a car accident.

   _____

   _____

   _____

2. In what ways does the text support the idea that Ponyboy is a worrier?

   _____

   _____

3. In the last paragraph, Ponyboy describes both of his brothers as nonhuman, but in very different ways. Explain this comparison using the text.

   _____

   _____

   _____

   _____

4. Ponyboy thinks Soda is wrong about Darry loving him. Based on the text, why does Ponyboy feel the need to lie to himself?

   _____

   _____

   _____

Name _____

Date _____

Making Connections–Social Class Dynamics

Directions: No matter the time or place, there have always been dynamics between different classes of people. Take time to ask family and friends about their experiences with the things that divide society. Then, use their experiences and your own ideas to answer the questions below about how the community problems in this story transcend time and place.

1. Why is society marked by class divisions? Are these divisions justified?

_____

_____

_____

_____

_____

2. What benefits can come from talking about these societal divisions?

_____

_____

_____

_____

_____

3. How do class divisions today differ from the divisions between the Socs and greasers in *The Outsiders*? In what ways are they the same?

_____

_____

_____

_____

_____

_____

Name _____

Date _____

Creating with the Story Elements

Directions: Thinking about the story elements of character, setting, and plot in a novel is very important to understanding what is happening and why. Complete **one** of the following activities based on what you've read so far. Be creative and have fun!

Characters

Select a character from the first two chapters and create any type of social media page for that character using real media or paper. What kinds of things would this character post, and what comments would be made about those posts from other characters? Use the text as a guide to create at least four posts with multiple comments.

Setting

If this story were told today, how would the following elements change? Make a before-and-after chart showing the differences.

- Socs vs. greasers
- Corvairs and Mustangs
- social hangout places
- names of characters
- how they "fight" one another

Plot

Towards the end of chapter 2, Ponyboy thinks that the Socs have it made. But the chapter ends with him saying, "I know better now." Imagine that for one day, Ponyboy wakes up as a Soc instead of a greaser. How would his life be different for this one day? Create two journal entries in Ponyboy's voice, one written from his normal perspective as a greaser and the other written on the day he is a Soc.

Vocabulary Overview

Ten key words from this section are provided below with definitions and sentences about how the words are used in the book. Choose one of the vocabulary activity sheets (pages 25 or 26) for students to complete as they read this section. Monitor students as they work to ensure the definitions they have found are accurate and relate to the text. Finally, discuss these important vocabulary words with students. If you think these words or other words in the section warrant more time devoted to them, there are suggestions in the introduction for other vocabulary activities (page 5).

Word or Phrase	Definition	Sentence about Text
rat race (ch. 3)	a lifestyle where one is constantly striving for money or power	Cherry thinks **rat race** is the perfect term to describe the Soc's life of constant acquisition.
cunning (ch. 3)	cleverly deceptive	Dallas has used his natural intelligence to become a **cunning** criminal.
the chips are down (ch. 3)	when things get really difficult	The greasers feel as if **the chips are** always **down** for them.
soused (ch. 3)	drunk	Two-Bit realizes he is **soused** because he asks for a Soc's phone number.
quavered (ch. 4)	shook	Johnny's voice **quavers** when he tells Ponyboy about what happened after he passed out at the park.
crocked (ch. 4)	drunk	After hosting a party all night, Buck Merril is **crocked**.
premonition (ch. 4)	a feeling that something is going to happen	The spooky church gives Ponyboy a **premonition** that something bad is going to happen.
gallant (ch. 5)	brave; heroic	Ponyboy is surprised when Johnny compares the **gallant** soldiers in *Gone with the Wind* to their hoodlum friend Dallas.
fiend (ch. 5)	a person who craves something	At home, Ponyboy drinks soda like a **fiend**.
green around the gills (ch. 5)	looking ill or nauseated	Ponyboy and Johnny get a little **green around the gills** when Dally drives the car too fast.

Name _____

Date _____

Understanding Vocabulary Words

Directions: The following words appear in this section of the book. Use context clues and reference materials to determine an accurate definition for each word.

Word or Phrase	Definition
rat race (ch. 3)	
cunning (ch. 3)	
the chips are down (ch. 3)	
soused (ch. 3)	
quavered (ch. 4)	
crocked (ch. 4)	
premonition (ch. 4)	
gallant (ch. 5)	
fiend (ch. 5)	
green around the gills (ch. 5)	

Name _____

Date _____

During-Reading Vocabulary Activity

Directions: As you read these chapters, record at least eight important words on the lines below. Try to find interesting, difficult, intriguing, special, or funny words. Your words can be long or short. They can be hard or easy to spell. After each word, use context clues in the text and reference materials to define the word.

- _____
- _____
- _____
- _____
- _____
- _____
- _____
- _____
- _____
- _____

Directions: Respond to the following questions about the words in this section.

1. Ponyboy uses words like **soused** and **crocked** to describe the drunken teens. How does the abuse of alcohol contribute to the tragic events in the park?

_____

_____

2. Why does the spiderwebby church give Ponyboy a feeling of **premonition**?

_____

_____

Analyzing the Literature

Provided below are discussion questions you can use in small groups, with the whole class, or for written assignments. Each question is given at two levels so you can choose the right question for each group of students. Activity sheets with these questions are provided (pages 28–29) if you want students to write their responses. For each question, a few key discussion points are provided for your reference.

Story Element	■ Level 1	▲ Level 2	Key Discussion Points
Character	Ponyboy says the greasers feel too passionately and the Socs don't feel at all. Use the text to describe if this is a fair statement.	Ponyboy says that it is not just money but rather feelings that separate the two classes. Use the text to describe if this is a fair statement.	Students should point to various scenes in the story to support their answers. Contradictory to this statement is how Cherry lets down her guard and how Johnny keeps all his emotions inside before the murder.
Setting	Since they both see the same sunset, Ponyboy realizes that his world and Cherry's world are not so different. In what ways is this true or not true?	What realization gives Ponyboy the idea that the worlds of the Socs and greasers are not so different? Is that true? Defend your answer with text references.	Students can fall on either side of the argument about the sunset, but they should use examples from the text to show either how the two worlds are different or not different.
Character	Cherry says she won't talk to Ponyboy at school but that it is not personal. Does it have to be that way? Explain your answer.	Cherry says she can't associate with Ponyboy at school, and he replies, "It's okay." Use the text to explain if it is really "okay" with him.	The social dynamics at their school prevent them from hanging out together. Based on events in the story, have students surmise what might happen at school if Ponyboy and Cherry socialized together.
Plot	How does the phrase, "Nothing gold can stay," apply to Johnny and Ponyboy?	Ponyboy knows he is missing some meaning of Robert Frost's "Nothing Gold Can Stay." What do you think he should take from the poem?	Students should see the connection of how Johnny and Ponyboy's young lives will never be the same after the murder. The "golden" lives they had, even with their hardships, are over.

Name _____

Date _____

■ Analyzing the Literature

Directions: Think about the section you just read. Read each question and provide a response that includes textual evidence.

1. Ponyboy says that the greasers feel too passionately and the Socs don't feel at all. Use the text to describe if this is a fair statement.

   _____

   _____

   _____

2. Since they both see the same sunset, Ponyboy realizes that his world and Cherry's world are not so different. In what ways is this true or not true?

   _____

   _____

   _____

3. Cherry says she won't talk to Ponyboy at school but that it is not personal. Does it have to be that way? Explain your answer.

   _____

   _____

   _____

4. How does the phrase, "Nothing gold can stay," apply to Johnny and Ponyboy?

   _____

   _____

   _____

▲ Analyzing the Literature

Directions: Think about the section you just read. Read each question and provide a response that includes textual evidence.

1. Ponyboy says that it is not just money but rather feelings that separate the two classes. Use the text to describe if this is a fair statement.

   _____

   _____

   _____

2. What realization gives Ponyboy the idea that the worlds of the Socs and greasers are not so different? Is that true? Defend your answer with text references.

   _____

   _____

   _____

3. Cherry says she can't associate with Ponyboy at school, and he replies, "It's okay." Use the text to explain if it is really "okay" with him.

   _____

   _____

   _____

4. Ponyboy knows he is missing some meaning of Robert Frost's poem "Nothing Gold Can Stay." What do you think he should take from the poem?

   _____

   _____

   _____

   _____

Name _____

Date _____

Reader Response

Directions: Choose one of the following prompts about this section to answer. Be sure you include a topic sentence in your response, use textual evidence to support your opinion, and provide a strong conclusion that summarizes your opinion.

Writing Prompts

- **Argument Piece**—Choose one Soc character and one greaser character from the novel. Defend why you think you three could all be friends. Support your argument by describing personality characteristics mentioned in the text that the three of you have in common.
- **Narrative Piece**—Choose a scene and rewrite it from the point of view of a character other than Ponyboy. Use the same writing style as S.E. Hinton, but write in the new character's voice rather than Ponyboy's voice.

_____

_____

_____

_____

_____

_____

_____

_____

_____

_____

_____

_____

_____

_____

Name _____

Date _____

Close Reading the Literature

Directions: Closely reread the section in chapter 5 beginning with, "I woke up late that night." Stop reading with, "Dally was so real he scared me." Read each question and then revisit the text to find evidence that supports your answer.

1. After crying so much, Ponyboy finally relaxes and knows that he can take whatever happens next. Use the text to explain how and why he comes to this realization.

   _____

   _____

   _____

2. Ponyboy is surprised to find that Johnny is a deep thinker. Give examples from the text to show why Ponyboy realizes this is true.

   _____

   _____

   _____

3. Ponyboy is surprised to hear Johnny describe Dally as "gallant." Use the text to explain why Johnny holds this surprising opinion.

   _____

   _____

   _____

4. Why does Ponyboy prefer books, clouds, and sunsets to "real life"?

   _____

   _____

   _____

Name _____

Date _____

Making Connections—It's All in Perspective

Directions: Talk to at least three people to find out their perspectives on a specific topic of your choosing (such as using social media in schools). Then, use what you have learned about other people's perspectives to draw a cartoon about the topic.

Name

Date

Creating with the Story Elements

Directions: Thinking about the story elements of character, setting, and plot in a novel is very important to understanding what is happening and why. Complete **one** of the following activities based on what you've read so far. Be creative and have fun!

Characters

Create a cover for a comic book featuring Soda, Two-Bit, and Darry as superheroes who exhibit the qualities described by Ponyboy in chapter 5.

Setting

If Ponyboy and Johnny could have had a playlist to listen to while waiting at the church, which songs would be on that playlist? Make a playlist of at least 10 songs and explain the reason for each song's inclusion. Support your reasons with references to the text.

Plot

Create an image (digital, collage, drawing, or painting) that illustrates the Robert Frost poem, "Nothing Gold Can Stay" and how it relates to this story. Include a written explanation of your creation.

Vocabulary Overview

Ten key words from this section are provided below with definitions and sentences about how the words are used in the book. Choose one of the vocabulary activity sheets (pages 35 or 36) for students to complete as they read this section. Monitor students as they work to ensure the definitions they have found are accurate and relate to the text. Finally, discuss these important vocabulary words with students. If you think these words or other words in the section warrant more time devoted to them, there are suggestions in the introduction for other vocabulary activities (page 5).

Word or Phrase	Definition	Sentence about Text
give a hang (ch. 6)	care; show concern	Johnny's parents don't **give a hang** what happens to him.
blast it (ch. 6)	an exclamation of frustration	"**Blast it**, Johnny, why didn't you think of turning yourself in five days ago?"
beefed him (ch. 6)	bothered him	When something really **beefs him**, he doesn't stay quiet about it.
give a Yankee dime (ch. 6)	did not care	Dally usually doesn't **give a Yankee dime** about what other people do, he only cares about himself.
weed-fiend (ch. 6)	smoking addict	Ponyboy smokes so much they call him the **weed-fiend** of his family.
lousy (ch. 6)	miserable; bad	He feels **lousy** about reminding Johnny of his home situation.
palomino (ch. 7)	horse with a golden body and white tail and mane	Ponyboy compares his charismatic brother Sodapop to a **palomino** colt.
juvenile delinquents (ch. 7)	people under the age of 18 who break the law	The **juvenile delinquents** do an unexpected thing when they save the children from the fire.
cocksure (ch. 7)	arrogantly confident	Steve has a **cocksure** attitude about his ability to handle problems.
exploits (ch. 7)	bold and daring feats	Two-Bit likes to describe his many **exploits** to Ponyboy.

Understanding Vocabulary Words

Directions: The following words appear in this section of the book. Use context clues and reference materials to determine an accurate definition for each word.

Word or Phrase	Definition
give a hang (ch. 6)	
blast it (ch. 6)	
beefed him (ch. 6)	
give a Yankee dime (ch. 6)	
weed-fiend (ch. 6)	
lousy (ch. 6)	
palomino (ch. 7)	
juvenile delinquents (ch. 7)	
cocksure (ch. 7)	
exploits (ch. 7)	

Name _____

Date _____

During-Reading Vocabulary Activity

Directions: As you read these chapters, record at least eight important words on the lines below. Try to find interesting, difficult, intriguing, special, or funny words. Your words can be long or short. They can be hard or easy to spell. After each word, use context clues in the text and reference materials to define the word.

- _____
- _____
- _____
- _____
- _____
- _____
- _____
- _____
- _____
- _____

Directions: Now, organize your words. Rewrite each of your words on a sticky note. Work as a group to create a bar graph of your words. You should stack any words that are the same on top of one another. Different words appear in different columns. Finally, discuss with your group why certain words were chosen more often than other words.

Analyzing the Literature

Provided below are discussion questions you can use in small groups, with the whole class, or for written assignments. Each question is given at two levels so you can choose the right question for each group of students. Activity sheets with these questions are provided (pages 38–39) if you want students to write their responses. For each question, a few key discussion points are provided for your reference.

Story Element	■ Level 1	▲ Level 2	Key Discussion Points
Character	How does Johnny seem to change when he helps the kids out of the fire?	Why would rescuing children from the fire bring out a different side of Johnny that no one has ever seen?	Helping others helps people like Johnny feel that they are valued, have a purpose in life, and can fill a need in society. Johnny may also feel joy and relief at letting go of his usual persistent fears and showing true bravery.
Plot	Why does Ponyboy feel that he is home when he hugs his brothers at the hospital?	What does Ponyboy realize about Darry when the two embrace at the hospital? Why does he say that he is "finally home"?	Compare Johnny's home life to Ponyboy's home life. Talk about how Ponyboy is able to forgive Darry for hitting him because he finally sees him as a real (flawed) human and realizes that much of Darry's strictness comes from love and concern.
Setting	If Ponyboy, Soda, and Darry are made to live apart, will it be a positive or negative change, or both?	What major life changes might occur if the courts separate Ponyboy, Soda, and Darry?	They might not see each other because of work schedules. Soda might have to go back to school. Discuss how Ponyboy might end up in a place like Johnny's home where he doesn't really belong.
Character	How does his conversation with Randy change the way Ponyboy thinks about Socs?	Randy indicates that he would rather leave town than go to the rumble. Why does he feel so desperate?	Discuss Cherry's words about things being rough all over. Talk about why Randy decides to open up to Ponyboy and what he might end up doing. Discuss whether or not Ponyboy will defend the Socs in some way.

Name _____

Date _____

■ Analyzing the Literature

Directions: Think about the section you just read. Read each question and provide a response that includes textual evidence.

1. How does Johnny seem to change when he helps the kids out of the fire?

_____

_____

_____

2. Why does Ponyboy feel that he is home when he hugs his brothers at the hospital?

_____

_____

_____

3. If Ponyboy, Soda, and Darry are made to live apart, will it be a positive or negative change, or both?

_____

_____

_____

_____

4. How does his conversation with Randy change the way Ponyboy thinks about Socs?

_____

_____

_____

_____

Name _____

Date _____

▲ Analyzing the Literature

Directions: Think about the section you just read. Read each question and provide a response that includes textual evidence.

1. Why would rescuing children from the fire bring out a different side of Johnny that no one has ever seen?

_____

_____

_____

_____

2. What does Ponyboy realize about Darry when the two embrace at the hospital? Why does he say that he is "finally home"?

_____

_____

_____

_____

3. What major life changes might occur if the courts separate Ponyboy, Soda, and Darry?

_____

_____

_____

4. Randy indicates that he would rather leave town than go to the rumble. Why does he feel so desperate?

_____

_____

_____

Name _____

Date _____

Reader Response

Directions: Choose one of the following prompts about this section to answer. Be sure you include a topic sentence in your response, use textual evidence to support your opinion, and provide a strong conclusion that summarizes your opinion.

Writing Prompts

- **Narrative Piece**—Ponyboy, Johnny, and Dally are very brave during the fire at the church. Write about any real-life situations that this scene reminds you of.
- **Informative/Explanatory**—Choose a paragraph from the text that you think is well written. Describe why you like the writing in this particular paragraph.

_____

_____

_____

_____

_____

_____

_____

_____

_____

_____

_____

_____

_____

_____

_____

Name _____

Date _____

Close Reading the Literature

Directions: Closely reread the section in chapter 7 that begins with, "I glanced at Two-Bit." Read to the end of the chapter. Read each question below and then revisit the text to find evidence that supports your answer.

1. Use details from the text to describe why Ponyboy insists that being a greaser has nothing to do with "playing hero."

   _____

   _____

   _____

2. Were Cherry's words about the Socs being "too cool to feel anything" true? What text helps you understand what Ponyboy thinks about this?

   _____

   _____

   _____

3. Randy thinks that all Bob wanted was for someone to say "no" to him. According to the text, what difference would this have made in his life?

   _____

   _____

   _____

   _____

4. Ponyboy tells Randy that once a person gets a little money, he hates the whole world. What does he mean by this? Defend your answer with references to the text.

   _____

   _____

   _____

   _____

Name _____

Date _____

Making Connections–Difficult Family Situations

Directions: Many people live in situations like Johnny's home. Read the questions, do some research, and answer the questions below.

1. How do the descriptions of Johnny's home life help you to feel compassion for real children in these types of circumstances?

   _____

   _____

   _____

   _____

   _____

2. What are tangible things that everyday people can do to help those who are caught in difficult family situations? Create a list of things students your age can do to make a difference.

   _____

   _____

   _____

   _____

   _____

3. Find out where the nearest shelter or children's home is located. What are some things this place needs, and how can students your age help out?

   _____

   _____

   _____

   _____

   _____

Name _____

Date _____

Creating with the Story Elements

Directions: Thinking about the story elements of character, setting, and plot in a novel is very important to understanding what is happening and why. Complete **one** of the following activities based on what you've read so far. Be creative and have fun!

Characters

Tell the story of going to the hospital from Darry's perspective. What is he feeling and how is he coping with what has happened to his little brother? Write his side of the story and make an audio recording.

Setting

If Ponyboy's home situation had been different, how might events in the story have changed? Create a comic strip to show how the novel would be different if, for example, Ponyboy's parents were still alive.

Plot

Write the full newspaper article titled, "Juvenile Delinquents Turn Heroes." Tell the story from the exciting perspective of the outside world looking at two boys who unexpectedly became heroes.

Vocabulary Overview

Ten key words from this section are provided below with definitions and sentences about how the words are used in the book. Choose one of the vocabulary activity sheets (pages 45 or 46) for students to complete as they read this section. Monitor students as they work to ensure the definitions they have found are accurate and relate to the text. Finally, discuss these important vocabulary words with students. If you think these words or other words in the section warrant more time devoted to them, there are suggestions in the introduction for other vocabulary activities (page 5).

Word or Phrase	Definition	Sentence about Text
juiced up (ch. 8)	excited	Ponyboy tells Johnny not to get **juiced up** in the hospital or the doctor won't let them visit anymore.
no-count (ch. 8)	useless; without merit	Johnny's spiteful mother calls her son's friends "**no-count** hoodlums."
ornery (ch. 8)	mean; bad-tempered	Ponyboy knows Dally will be okay because he is acting like his usual **ornery** self.
panicky (ch. 8)	stricken with sudden, overwhelming fear	Ponyboy gets **panicky** when he thinks he might miss the rumble.
reformatory (ch. 9)	a school where young kids are sent instead of prison	Younger greasers might be sent to the **reformatory** for breaking the law.
skin rumble (ch. 9)	a fight without weapons	The Socs and the greasers plan a **skin rumble** so that no one will get seriously hurt in the fight.
menace (ch. 9)	threat	Many people think greasers are a **menace** to society because they are always getting into trouble.
blow at the first sign of trouble (ch. 9)	get out of the way; go away	To keep from being sent to a boy's home, Ponyboy is told to **blow at the first sign of trouble**.
ruefully (ch. 9)	mournfully; showing sadness	When he talks about his younger brother being sent to a reformatory, Tim grins **ruefully**.
detached (ch. 9)	disconnected	The adrenaline of the rumble allows Ponyboy to feel **detached** from the pain of his injuries.

Name _____

Date _____

Understanding Vocabulary Words

Directions: The following words appear in this section of the book. Use context clues and reference materials to determine an accurate definition for each word.

Word or Phrase	Definition
juiced up (ch. 8)	
no-count (ch. 8)	
ornery (ch. 8)	
panicky (ch. 8)	
reformatory (ch. 9)	
skin rumble (ch. 9)	
menace (ch. 9)	
blow at the first sign of trouble (ch. 9)	
ruefully (ch. 9)	
detached (ch. 9)	

Name _____

Date _____

During-Reading Vocabulary Activity

Directions: As you read these chapters, record at least eight important words on the lines below. Try to find interesting, difficult, intriguing, special, or funny words. Your words can be long or short. They can be hard or easy to spell. After each word, use context clues in the text and reference materials to define the word.

- _____
- _____
- _____
- _____
- _____
- _____
- _____
- _____

Directions: Respond to the following questions about the words in this section.

1. Explain why seeing Dally act like his usual **ornery** self in the hospital makes Ponyboy feel better.

   _____

   _____

2. Why does Tim Shepard grin **ruefully** when he talks about his younger brother being sent to the reformatory?

   _____

   _____

Analyzing the Literature

Provided below are discussion questions you can use in small groups, with the whole class, or for written assignments. Each question is given at two levels so you can choose the right question for each group of students. Activity sheets with these questions are provided (pages 48–49) if you want students to write their responses. For each question, a few key discussion points are provided for your reference.

Story Element	■ Level 1	▲ Level 2	Key Discussion Points
Character	Why does Two-Bit say that the gang could get along without anyone but Johnny? What makes Johnny so special?	Ponyboy understands that the gang needs Johnny just as much as he needs the gang . . . and for the same reason. What does this mean?	Johnny needs the gang to be his family, just as the gang considers Johnny to be a member of their family. They take care of him when his family doesn't. He fills the void for the gang by being the quiet, kind one and by listening to the others.
Character	Johnny does not want to see his mother. Why do you think that is?	In what ways is refusing to see his mother in the hospital a turning point for Johnny?	Earlier in the novel, Johnny is devastated that his parents have not asked about him when he is hiding out for a week. In the hospital, Johnny's resolve is to leave his parents behind and refuse to take any further abuse. Facing his mortality has made him stronger.
Setting	Johnny's life on the streets has been difficult in many ways. How does this make his injury even more tragic?	Ponyboy says 16 years on the streets can teach and show a person all the wrong things. What does he mean by this?	Ponyboy is grieving over the life that Johnny has had. He wants Johnny to experience the good in life. Ponyboy wishes that Johnny could have had a better life, and not so much sorrow and pain.
Plot	How does Cherry feel about Bob now that he is dead?	Why can't Cherry look at the person who killed Bob, even though she knows Johnny is a good kid?	Bob's good side was what Cherry loved. Discuss the differences between Johnny and Bob and how complicated the situation would have been if Bob had been the killer.

Name _____

Date _____

Analyzing the Literature

Directions: Think about the section you just read. Read each question and provide a response that includes textual evidence.

1. Why does Two-Bit say that the gang could get along without anyone but Johnny? What makes Johnny so special?

   _____

   _____

   _____

   _____

2. Johnny does not want to see his mother. Why do you think that is?

   _____

   _____

   _____

   _____

3. Johnny's life on the streets has been difficult in many ways. How does this make his injury even more tragic?

   _____

   _____

   _____

   _____

4. How does Cherry feel about Bob now that he is dead?

   _____

   _____

   _____

Name _____

Date _____

▲ Analyzing the Literature

Directions: Think about the section you just read. Read each question and provide a response that includes textual evidence.

1. Ponyboy understands that the gang needs Johnny just as much as he needs the gang . . . and for the same reason. What does this mean?

   _____

   _____

   _____

2. In what ways is refusing to see his mother in the hospital a turning point for Johnny?

   _____

   _____

   _____

3. Ponyboy says 16 years on the streets can teach and show a person all the wrong things. What does he mean by this?

   _____

   _____

   _____

4. Why can't Cherry look at the person who killed Bob, even though she knows Johnny is a good kid?

   _____

   _____

   _____

Name _____

Date _____

Reader Response

Directions: Choose one of the following prompts about this section to answer. Be sure you include a topic sentence in your response, use textual evidence to support your opinion, and provide a strong conclusion that summarizes your opinion.

Writing Prompts

- **Narrative Piece**—Johnny's parents don't seem to care that he goes missing for a week. On the other hand, Ponyboy's brothers are worried sick. Imagine that you take off with a friend for a week. Write a scene that describes the reunion with your family upon your return.
- **Informative/Explanatory Piece**—Choose a Soc and a greaser, and explain how they are the same and different. As you compare them, think about how they might be if they each lived in the opposite part of town.

_____

_____

_____

_____

_____

_____

_____

_____

_____

_____

_____

_____

_____

Name _____

Date _____

Close Reading the Literature

Directions: Closely reread the section in chapter 9 beginning with, "I went back to stand with Soda . . . ." Stop with, "they shouldn't hate . . . ." Read each question below and then revisit the text to find evidence that supports your answer.

1. Use the text to discuss why people usually go by looks, even though they shouldn't, when judging people's motives.

   _____

   _____

   _____

2. The text says that Darry's eyes flicker and then go back to ice again. Why does Darry have to keep his eyes cold and hard?

   _____

   _____

   _____

3. Ponyboy believes that only he and Soda recognize that Darry is ashamed to be a greaser. What textual evidence explains this?

   _____

   _____

   _____

   _____

4. Ponyboy says that both Paul and Darry should know better than to fight, that they are supposed to be smarter than that. Based on the events in the story, why do you think they come to fight anyway?

   _____

   _____

   _____

   _____

Name _____

Date _____

Making Connections—Jack London's Wolves

Directions: Find out about how wolves fight by watching videos or reading materials about wolves. Read a summary of the Jack London novels *Call of the Wild* and *White Fang* that Ponyboy mentions in chapter 9. Both of these novels deal with wolf fights. Then, using the T-chart below, make comparisons between the gangs in *The Outsiders* and wolves in real life.

Gangs in *The Outsiders*	Wolves

Name _____

Date _____

Creating with the Story Elements

Directions: Thinking about the story elements of character, setting, and plot in a novel is very important to understanding what is happening and why. Complete **one** of the following activities based on what you've read so far. Be creative and have fun!

Characters

Dally tells Ponyboy to get tough so he won't get hurt and to look out for himself so nothing will touch him. What is Dally really trying to say to Ponyboy? Is this good advice for Ponyboy? Write a letter from Ponyboy to an advice column asking for help understanding Dally. Then write a letter back to him as the advice expert.

Setting

The big fight takes place at a vacant lot under street lamps. What other places would be fitting locations for this kind of fight, and how might the new setting change the outcome of the fight? Give at least three new scenarios and their consequences. Use pictures or drawings to show your ideas along with your written explanations.

Plot

Johnny's last words are to tell Ponyboy to stay gold. What does Johnny mean by this and why is it fitting that these would be his last words? Create a blog post from Johnny in the hospital. In this post, have Johnny talk about those words and Robert Frost's poem in relation to Ponyboy.

Vocabulary Overview

Ten key words from this section are provided below with definitions and sentences about how the words are used in the book. Choose one of the vocabulary activity sheets (pages 55 or 56) for students to complete as they read this section. Monitor students as they work to ensure the definitions they have found are accurate and relate to the text. Finally, discuss these important vocabulary words with students. If you think these words or other words in the section warrant more time devoted to them, there are suggestions in the introduction for other vocabulary activities (page 5).

Word or Phrase	Definition	Sentence about Text
dryly (ch. 10)	matter-of-factly	Ponyboy doesn't even realize he is bleeding until the man tells him **dryly**.
wreck (ch. 10)	an old, beaten-up car	The **wreck** has been through a lot, which is unlike the Socs' fancy cars.
grim (ch. 10)	uninviting	Dally's face has a look of **grim** triumph when he is shot by the police.
delirious (ch. 10)	not able to think or speak clearly	Ponyboy cannot remember what he said when he was **delirious**.
indignantly (ch. 10)	angrily; feeling insulted	Soda looks at Darry **indignantly** when he is instructed to take it easy on Ponyboy.
racked up (ch. 11)	upset; unstable	After Johnny's death, Ponyboy is all **racked up** emotionally.
lousing up (ch. 12)	messing up; ruining	In the months that follow the deaths, Ponyboy **louses up** his grades at school.
living in a vacuum (ch. 12)	cut off; separated; isolated	Darry worries because Ponyboy is **living in a vacuum** and not responding to the world around him.
what's the sweat (ch. 12)	what's the worry or concern	Even though he is failing English class, Ponyboy asks **what's the sweat** about his homework.
beefs (ch. 12)	complaints; arguments	Johnny was quiet and everyone in the gang brought their **beefs** to him.

Name _____

Date _____

Understanding Vocabulary Words

Directions: The following words appear in this section of the book. Use context clues and reference materials to determine an accurate definition for each word.

Word or Phrase	Definition
dryly (ch. 10)	
wreck (ch. 10)	
grim (ch. 10)	
delirious (ch. 10)	
indignantly (ch. 10)	
racked up (ch. 11)	
lousing up (ch. 12)	
living in a vacuum (ch. 12)	
what's the sweat (ch. 12)	
beefs (ch. 12)	

Name _____

Date _____

During-Reading Vocabulary Activity

Directions: As you read these chapters, choose five important words from the story. Use these words to complete the word flow chart below. On each arrow, write a word. In each box, explain how the connected pair of words relates to each other. An example for the words *racked up* and *louses up* has been done for you.

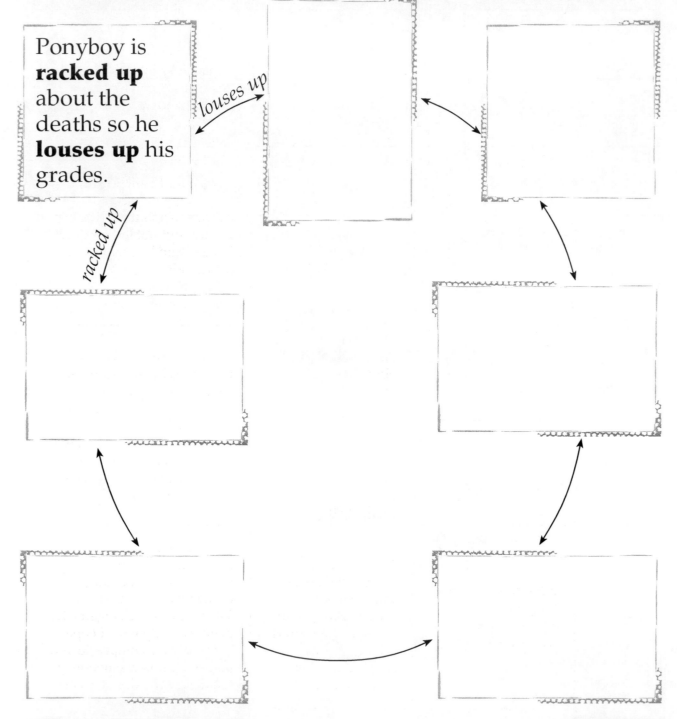

Ponyboy is **racked up** about the deaths so he **louses up** his grades.

louses up

racked up

Analyzing the Literature

Provided below are discussion questions you can use in small groups, with the whole class, or for written assignments. Each question is given at two levels so you can choose the right question for each group of students. Activity sheets with these questions are provided (pages 58–59) if you want students to write their responses. For each question, a few key discussion points are provided for your reference.

Story Element	■ Level 1	▲ Level 2	Key Discussion Points
Setting	At first, Ponyboy doesn't believe Johnny is dead. Why doesn't he accept what has happened?	How does Ponyboy's initial refusal to accept Johnny's death help him cope with what happened?	Ponyboy is in shock and denial after Johnny's death. This is common for many people who have lost people they love. It allows the brain to slowly accept the news.
Character	What effect did Bob's death have on Randy?	Ponyboy doesn't understand what Randy could have to lose. Use the text to explain what Randy could lose.	Randy, for the first time, is feeling remorse and confusion about his life. He cares about not letting down his dad and he cares about his friends. He, just like Ponyboy, has worries and fears about the future.
Character	Why does Soda want Ponyboy and Darry to stop fighting so much?	Soda is distressed about his brothers arguing. He says that they will end up like Dally before he died, which was worse than being dead. What does he mean?	Soda feels pulled in both directions by his brothers. He knows they need to love and cherish each other or they will become hard. Dally had hardened and was untouchable before he died. While he loved Johnny, he lived for himself.
Plot	What message does Ponyboy hope to convey when he writes his story?	After getting Johnny's note, Ponyboy realizes that he has a message to give to others. How could telling his story help change his community?	Ponyboy wants to remind people not to judge others when they do not really know what they are like. Viewpoints are changed when people openly talk. People become more compassionate and sympathetic when they see the other sides of a story.

Name _____

Date _____

■ Analyzing the Literature

Directions: Think about the section you just read. Read each question and provide a response that includes textual evidence.

1. At first, Ponyboy doesn't believe Johnny is dead. Why doesn't he accept what has happened?

_____

_____

_____

_____

2. What effect did Bob's death have on Randy?

_____

_____

_____

_____

3. Why does Soda want Ponyboy and Darry to stop fighting so much?

_____

_____

_____

_____

4. What message does Ponyboy hope to convey when he writes his story?

_____

_____

_____

_____

▲ Analyzing the Literature

Directions: Think about the section you just read. Read each question and provide a response that includes textual evidence.

1. How does Ponyboy's initial refusal to accept Johnny's death help him cope with what happened?

   _____

   _____

   _____

2. Ponyboy doesn't understand what Randy could possibly have to lose. Use the text to explain what Randy could lose.

   _____

   _____

   _____

3. Soda is distressed about his brothers arguing. He says that they will end up like Dally before he died, which was worse than being dead. What does he mean?

   _____

   _____

   _____

4. After getting Johnny's note, Ponyboy realizes that he has a message to give to others. How could telling his story help change his community?

   _____

   _____

   _____

   _____

Name _____

Date _____

Reader Response

Directions: Choose one of the following prompts about this section to answer. Be sure you include a topic sentence in your response, use textual evidence to support your opinion, and provide a strong conclusion that summarizes your opinion.

Writing Prompts

- **Argument Piece**—In what ways have you personally changed after reading this novel? When you think about your community, do you view situations differently?

- **Informative/Explanatory Piece**—Compare a character from this novel to a character from another work of fiction (a novel, a play, a film, or a short story). Which character do you admire more and why?

_____

_____

_____

_____

_____

_____

_____

_____

_____

_____

_____

_____

_____

_____

Close Reading the Literature

Directions: Closely reread the section in chapter 12 beginning with, "Ponyboy, I asked the nurse . . . ." Read to the end of the chapter. Read each question below and then revisit the text to find evidence that supports your answer.

1. According to the letter, Johnny is okay with the fact that he's dying. Why did Johnny change his views on life and death?

_____

_____

_____

2. In what ways is watching a sunset a symbol of being "gold" to Johnny?

_____

_____

_____

3. Johnny makes three references to Dally in his letter. What is the significance of this and what does it tell us about how Johnny felt about Dally?

_____

_____

_____

_____

4. Ponyboy realizes that his story is too vast of a problem to be just a personal thing. How does he know this, and what does he decide to do?

_____

_____

_____

_____

Name _____

Date _____

Making Connections—The Real Outsiders

Directions: Think about the book in its entirety and what you will take away as its main message. Then, answer the questions below.

1. What important message did the author hope to give by writing this book?

_____

_____

_____

_____

2. In what ways do the outsiders in this story represent many kinds of outsiders?

_____

_____

_____

_____

3. Who are the outsiders in your society? Explain their challenges.

_____

_____

_____

_____

_____

_____

_____

Name _____

Date _____

Creating with the Story Elements

Directions: Thinking about the story elements of character, setting, and plot in a novel is very important to understanding what is happening and why. Complete **one** of the following activities based on what you've read so far. Be creative and have fun!

Characters

Consider the three people Ponyboy remembers at the end of the story (Bob, Dally, and Johnny) and create a comic strip for each character showing a day in his life. In a fourth comic strip, show their worlds colliding and what happens as a result.

Setting

How would the novel *The Outsiders* change if it were to take place in your neighborhood today? Write a description of this in a writing style that is similar to Ponyboy's style. Then draw pictures, take photographs, or use downloaded images to illustrate your description.

Plot

Johnny tells Ponyboy to stay gold, but Robert Frost wrote, "nothing gold can stay." Was Robert Frost wrong when he wrote this? Write a letter to Frost that either agrees or disagrees with his poem.

Name _____

Date _____

Post-Reading Theme Thoughts

Directions: Read each of the statements in the first column. Choose a main character from *The Outsiders*. Think about that character's point of view. From that character's perspective, decide if the character would agree or disagree with the statements. Record the character's opinion by marking an X in Agree or Disagree for each statement. Explain your choices in the fourth column using text evidence.

Character I Chose: _____

Statement	Agree	Disagree	Explain Your Answer
Rich people have just as many worries as poor people.			
It is better to grow up too fast than to be treated like a child.			
People judge others by their appearances.			
Sometimes, life isn't fair.			

Culminating Activity:
Two Viewpoints

Directions: Choose one greaser and one Soc from the story. Based on what you learned as you read this novel, compare and contrast their viewpoints about the importance of the following topics.

Topic	Soc: _____'s Viewpoint	Greaser: _____'s Viewpoint
loyalty to friends		
relationships with family		
a sense of belonging		
maintaining status		
doing the right thing		

Name _____

Date _____

Culminating Activity:
Two Viewpoints (cont.)

Directions: Ponyboy's story has been published. A movie based on the book will be coming soon, and advertisers are anxious to get the word out. Now that you understand differing viewpoints (the Socs and the greasers), a marketing company has come to you for help. Since many people in these groups see things differently, the marketing company needs to design specific advertisements for the Socs and specific advertisements for the greasers. Decide what will attract each group to the movie and then choose one of the following projects to complete for the marketing company.

- Create two poster advertisements for the story. One will be to draw in the Socs and the other one will be to attract the greasers. Make sure your visuals are bold and bright!

- Create two movie trailers for the story. One will be to draw in the Socs and the other one will be to attract the greasers.

- Create two social media pages to advertise the movie. One will be to draw in the Socs and the other one will be to attract the greasers.

Name _____

Date _____

Comprehension Assessment

Directions: Circle the letter for the best response to each question.

1. What statement best explains the main reason the greasers are so bitter towards the Socs?

   A. The Socs have good families.

   B. The Socs have all the breaks in life.

   C. The Socs are the best fighters.

   D. The Socs have better friends.

2. What detail from the novel provides the best evidence for your answer to number 1?

   E. "He was the best buddy a guy ever had. I mean, he was a good fighter and tuff and everything, but he was a real person too."

   F. "And tonight . . . people get hurt in rumbles, maybe killed. I'm sick of it because it doesn't do any good."

   G. "You can't win, even if you whip us. You'll still be where you were before—at the bottom. And we'll still be the lucky ones."

   H. "I mean, most parents would be proud of a kid like that—good lookin' and smart and everything, but they gave in to him all the time."

3. What is the main idea of the text below?

   _____

   _____

   _____

   _____

   "Darry love me? I thought of those hard, pale eyes. Soda was wrong for once, I thought. Darry doesn't love anyone or anything, except maybe Soda. I didn't hardly think of him as being human. I don't care, I lied to myself, I don't care about him either. Soda's enough, and I'd have him until I got out of school. I don't care about Darry. But I was still lying and I knew it. I lie to myself all the time. But I never believe me."

Comprehension Assessment (cont.)

4. Which **two** details support your answer to question 3?

   A. Ponyboy really does love his brother Darry, but it hurts to admit it.

   B. Ponyboy believes Darry only sees him as another mouth to feed.

   C. Darry does not act human.

   D. Ponyboy cares how Darry feels about him.

5. Which statement best supports how Johnny feels toward his family?

   E. Johnny feels indifferent toward his family's behavior.

   F. Johnny is angry and hateful toward his family.

   G. Johnny doesn't care about his family because he has the gang.

   H. Johnny is hurt because his family does not want him.

6. What is the meaning of "Nothing Gold Can Stay" by Robert Frost?

   _____

   _____

   _____

7. Which statement best expresses a central theme of the novel?

   A. Appreciate your friends while you still have them.

   B. You can be whatever you want to be.

   C. Don't hang out with the wrong kind of people.

   D. Don't judge a person by what he or she looks like.

8. What detail provides the best evidence for your answer to number 7?

   E. "Someone should tell their side of the story, and maybe people would understand then and wouldn't be so quick to judge a boy by the amount of hair oil he wore."

   F. "And don't be so bugged over being a greaser. You still have a lot of time to make yourself be what you want."

   G. "Like the way you dig sunsets, Pony. That's gold. Keep that way, it's a good way to be."

   H. "Johnny was something more than a buddy to all of us. I guess he had listened to more beefs and more problems from more people than any of us."

Name _____

Date _____

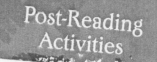

Response to Literature: Who Is the Outsider?

Directions: The novel is titled *The Outsiders* and tells the story of the conflicts between two groups of people. On the lines below, answer this central question: *Who are the real outsiders in this story?* Defend your answer with references from the text.

_____

_____

_____

_____

_____

_____

_____

_____

_____

_____

_____

_____

_____

_____

_____

_____

_____

Name _____

Date _____

Response to Literature Rubric

Directions: Use this rubric to evaluate student responses.

	Exceptional Writing	Quality Writing	Developing Writing
Focus and Organization	☐ States a clear opinion and elaborates well. Engages the reader from hook through the middle to the conclusion. Demonstrates clear understanding of the intended audience and purpose of the piece.	☐ Provides a clear and consistent opinion. Maintains a clear perspective and supports it through elaborating details. Makes the opinion clear in the opening hook and summarizes well in the conclusion.	☐ Provides an inconsistent point of view. Does not support the topic adequately or misses pertinent information. Provides lack of clarity in the beginning, middle, and conclusion.
Text Evidence	☐ Provides comprehensive and accurate support. Includes relevant and worthwhile text references.	☐ Provides limited support. Provides few supporting text references.	☐ Provides very limited support for the text. Provides no supporting text references.
Written Expression	☐ Uses descriptive and precise language with clarity and intention. Maintains a consistent voice and uses an appropriate tone that supports meaning. Uses multiple sentence types and transitions well between ideas.	☐ Uses a broad vocabulary. Maintains a consistent voice and supports a tone and feelings through language. Varies sentence length and word choices.	☐ Uses a limited and unvaried vocabulary. Provides an inconsistent or weak voice and tone. Provides little to no variation in sentence type and length.
Language Conventions	☐ Capitalizes, punctuates, and spells accurately. Demonstrates complete thoughts within sentences, with accurate subject-verb agreement. Uses paragraphs appropriately and with clear purpose.	☐ Capitalizes, punctuates, and spells accurately. Demonstrates complete thoughts within sentences and appropriate grammar. Paragraphs are properly divided and supported.	☐ Incorrectly capitalizes, punctuates, and spells. Uses fragmented or run-on sentences. Utilizes poor grammar overall. Paragraphs are poorly divided and developed.

The responses provided here are just examples of what students may answer. Many accurate responses are possible for the questions throughout this unit.

During-Reading Vocabulary Activity—Section 1: Chapters 1–2 (page 16)

1. Dally smiles **roguishly** because he is always getting into trouble and causing mischief.

2. They might use the word **heater** because guns make situations more intense or maybe because of the expression "packing heat."

Close Reading the Literature—Section 1: Chapters 1–2 (page 21)

1. Darry would have gone to college and possibly played football. He wouldn't have to have a job to support his family at this point in his life.

2. Ponyboy worries about why the Socs hate them so much. He worries about his brothers having to work so hard. He also worries that Darry doesn't love him.

3. Ponyboy sees Soda as a Greek god, but he sees Darry as nonfeeling with his cold eyes and lack of emotion.

4. Ponyboy lies to himself that he doesn't need Darry so he will not feel hurt and rejected, but he really does need him and wants his love and acceptance.

During-Reading Vocabulary Activity—Section 2: Chapters 3–5 (page 26)

1. The Socs are drunk, and they stop thinking through the consequences of their actions. They are aggressive and violent in ways they might not be if sober.

2. The church is cold and empty, and therefore, spooky. This feeling gives Ponyboy a **premonition** that bad things might happen there.

Close Reading the Literature—Section 2: Chapters 3–5 (page 31)

1. Ponyboy has to get used to the idea that his life is forever changed. Once he cries all he can, he is finally able to accept this. He also takes comfort that Johnny feels the same way.

2. Ponyboy realizes that Johnny can find meaning in parts of *Gone with the Wind* that Ponyboy did not see. He says that Johnny likes to explore new things when he learns about them.

3. Johnny explains that Dally would take the blame for others' bad deeds without saying anything or telling on them. Ponyboy realizes that Johnny sees Dally as a hero.

4. Ponyboy has a hard time facing real life, he prefers to live in his books and dream about possibilities. He is optimistic and can't handle the harshness of life.

Close Reading the Literature—Section 3: Chapters 6–7 (page 41)

1. Ponyboy insists that it is the individual, not the group, that makes a person. He points out that Two-Bit would not have saved the children.

2. From talking to Randy, Ponyboy realizes that Randy has deep feelings, but that he doesn't show them. Randy reaches out to Ponyboy because he feels that he can talk to Ponyboy honestly.

3. If a parent had told Bob no, Bob might not have taken chances and been so reckless. He would have been made to be responsible and do the right things instead of drinking and looking for fights. He might still be alive.

4. Perhaps Ponyboy realizes that money doesn't make people happy, so they hate the world when it doesn't make them happy. They look for something to blame. Ponyboy realizes that there are pressures everywhere, even in the lives of the Socs.

During-Reading Vocabulary Activity—Section 4: Chapters 8–9 (page 46)

1. Ponyboy realizes that Dally is not seriously injured because he is acting like his usual **ornery** self.

2. Tim grins **ruefully** because he misses his brother, and he is sorry he was sent away.

Close Reading the Literature—Section 4: Chapters 8–9 (page 51)

1. People see a clean cut boy and a greaser and assume the greaser did the crime just because of how he is dressed. His clothing makes him seem suspicious.

2. Darry has to keep his eyes as ice because he has to look tough. He can't afford to feel anything towards his old friend when he is getting ready to fight him.

3. As family, they know each other best, so he and Soda are able to pick up on Darry's feelings. Regardless if anyone else could pick up on those feelings, they are not part of the family, and it would not affect them in the same way.

4. Both Darry and Paul were educated and successful in school. They were athletes and knew how to work together as a team. Ponyboy feels that these factors should have stopped both of them from fighting. However, pride and group pressure bring them both to the rumble.

Close Reading the Literature—Section 5: Chapters 10–12 (page 61)

1. Johnny is okay with dying because he knows that he did something heroic in saving those children. Their parents even thanked him. Johnny knows those kids have a chance in life to be something with parents who support them like that.

2. Johnny sees watching the sunset as staying fresh and young in one's mind. It shows that Ponyboy appreciates the simple things in life and has hopes for the future.

3. Johnny wants Dally to know that he doesn't regret helping those children survive the fire, even if it means losing his own life. He also wants him to know that there is still hope for him to live a good life. By all these statements, Johnny shows that he cares for Dally and thinks of him all the time.

4. Ponyboy knows this because of the people he's met on both sides of the conflict. He knows that hearing his story can help save people a lot of heartache and keep them from making bad decisions. If they can hear the other side of the story, they might not jump to judge others by how they look.

Comprehension Assessment (pages 67–68)

1. B. The Socs have all the breaks in life.

2. G. "You can't win, even if you whip us. You'll still be where you were before—at the bottom. And we'll still be the lucky ones . . . ."

3. Main idea: Ponyboy cares how Darry feels about him even if he tells himself that it doesn't matter.

4. A. Ponyboy really does love his brother Darry, but it hurts to admit it. D. Ponyboy cares how Darry feels about him.

5. H. Johnny is hurt because his family does not want him.

6. The poem refers to the fact that the innocence of youth is hard to hold and eventually will pass.

7. D. Don't judge a person by what he or she looks like.

8. E. "Someone should tell their side of the story, and maybe people would understand then and wouldn't be so quick to judge a boy by the amount of hair oil he wore."